Carte des Frontieres
Françoises, et Angloises
dans le CANADA depuis
Montreal jusques au Fort
du Quesne

Engraved for Rogers Translation

LAC ONTARIO

NEW YORK
STYLE

Suzanne
SLESIN
Stafford
CLIFF
Daniel
ROZENSZTROCH

PHOTOGRAPHS BY
Gilles
DE CHABANEIX

FOREWORD BY
RICHARD F. SHEPARD

DESIGN BY
STAFFORD CLIFF

ART ASSOCIATE
IAN HAMMOND

CLARKSON POTTER/PUBLISHERS
NEW YORK

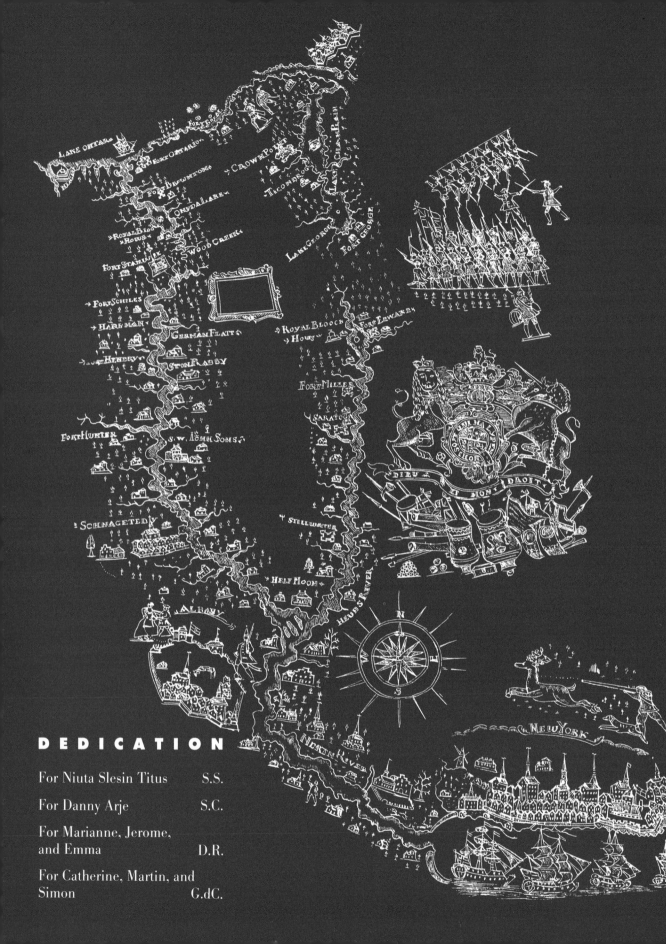

Copyright © 1992 by Suzanne Slesin.
Stafford Cliff. Daniel Rozensztroch. Gilles de
Chabaneix

All rights reserved. No part of this book may
be reproduced or transmitted in any form or
by any means. electronic or mechanical.
including photocopying. recording. or by any
information storage and retrieval system.
without permission in writing from the
publisher.

Published by Clarkson N. Potter. Inc..
201 East 50th Street. New York. New York
10022. Member of the Crown Publishing
Group.

CLARKSON N. POTTER. POTTER. and
colophon are trademarks of Clarkson N.
Potter. Inc.

Manufactured in Japan.

Library of Congress Cataloging-in-
Publication Data

Slesin. Suzanne.
    New York style / Suzanne Slesin.
Stafford Cliff. Daniel Rozensztroch :
photographs by Gilles de Chabaneix :
foreword by Richard Shepard. — 1st ed.
    Includes index
    1. Interior decoration—New York
(State)—Themes. motives.
I. Cliff. Stafford. II. Rozensztroch.
Daniel. III. De Chabaneix. Gilles.
IV. Title.
NK2002.S58   1992
747.2147—dc20   92-7502
                                 CIP

ISBN 0-517-58802-1

10 9 8 7 6 5 4 3 2 1

First Edition

ENDPAPERS: Aboriginal map of the present
territory of New York State. 1848. Courtesy
of The New-York Historical Society. N.Y.C.
OPPOSITE PAGES 1 AND 264: Carte des
Frontierres Françoises. 1799. Courtesy of
The New-York Historical Society. N.Y.C.
PAGE 1: Map of Nieu Nederlandt. c. 1614.
Courtesy of The New-York Historical
Society. N.Y.C. PAGES 2–3: A Mappe of
Colonel Romer's Voyage. 1700. Map Division.
The New York Public Library. Astor. Lenox
and Tilden Foundations. PAGES 4–5: Totius
Neobelgii Nova et Accuratissima Tabula. 1673.
Map Division. The New York Public Library.
Astor. Lenox and Tilden Foundations.
PAGES 6–7: Geological map of New York
State. By permission of the British Library.
PAGES 8–9: New York—The Empire
State. Courtesy of The New-York
Historical Society. N.Y.C.
PAGES 10–11: Photograph
available from the U.S. Department
of the Interior. U.S. Geological
Survey EROS Data Center.

DEDICATION

For Niuta Slesin Titus   S.S.

For Danny Arje   S.C.

For Marianne, Jerome,
and Emma   D.R.

For Catherine, Martin, and
Simon   G.dC.

ACKNOWLEDGMENTS

Thank you, thank you, thank you to all those who let us photograph in your homes and who helped us through *New York Style.*

You include James and Kathryn McLaughlin Abbe, Marion Adler, Lee Anderson, Kent and June Barwick, Jean-Paul Beaujard, Eric Boman, Craig Kilborn and Hallie Bond at the Adirondack Museum, Frank Brozyna, Mario Buatta, Diana Burroughs and Jason McCoy, Ellen Chesler and Matthew Mallow, Barbara Cohen and Judith Stonehill and Francis Morrone of New York Bound Bookshop, Joanne Creveling, Mary Jo Daniels, Jean de Machy, Martin Dinowitz, Ethel and Irving Distel-Malchman, Stephen Drucker at the Home Section of the *New York Times*, Peter Dubow, David Dunlap, Alice Eisen, Mary Emmerling, Ippolito Etro, Tom Fallon, Frank Faulkner, Michael Formica, David and Virginia and Lanny Fox, Frances McLaughlin Gill, Adelaide Griswald, David Hanks, Jan Hashey, Bob Heimstra, Alanna Heiss, Elizabeth Herz, Richard Iverson, Robert Jackson, Harvey Kaiser, Ivan and Marilynn Gelfman Karp, Jolie Kelter and Michael Malcé, Ken Kendrick and Owen Hartley, Robert Kinnaman and Brian Ramaekers, Trudy Kramer, Catherine Laroche, Yves Legrand, Erica Lennard, Rosi Levai, Joy and Robert K. Lewis, Patrick Martin, William and Claudia McNamee at The Point, Alain Mertens, Raymond Meyer, Judith and James Milne, Robert Del Monaco, Ted Muehling, Joseph Napoli, Priscilla Nixon, Paola Navone, Alexander Nixon, Sofia Parrenas, Howard and Mindy Partman, Mark Rabun, Nina and Greg Ramsey, Katia Ramsey and Howard Read, Rita Reif, Robert and Jane Kaplowitz Rosenblum, Jean and Budd Rowland, Kris Ruhs, Jim Ryan at Olana, John Ryman, Jacqueline Schnabel, Faith Scott, Jonathan Scott, Nick Smith, Clinton and Joe Standart, Michael and Jake and Lucie Steinberg, Dora Steinberg, Betty and Fred Sterzer, Alex and Sabina Streeter, Jane and John Stubbs, Caroline Tinè, Barbara Toll, Harry Van Dyke, Florence and Stephen Wagner, Paule Verchère, Lyn and Gib Vincent, Paul Walter, Billy Weaver, Selma Weiser, Marlene Wetherill, George Wey, and Marilyn White.

Thank you also to our agents, Lucy Kroll and Barbara Hogenson; and to Karen Kligerman, our editorial assistant; Jim Balcerski at the Environmental Research Institute of Michigan; Ian Hammond, our art associate; the Hormozis at Momento Print Ltd.; Tony Tortoroli and Bill Fentre at Campaign Colour; Maurice White at Character Photosetting Limited; Michael Adams, who researched the "New York Timeline"; and Emily Gwathmey and John Margolies, our deltiologists.

We are grateful as well to our supporting support group at Clarkson Potter, which includes our publisher, Michelle Sidrane; our editor-in-chief, Carol Southern; and our editor, Roy Finamore; as well as Kristen Behrens, Andrea Connolly, Joan Denman, Allan Eady, Lisa Keim, Howard Klein, and Susan Magrino.

Suzanne Slesin, New York
Stafford Cliff, London
Daniel Rozensztroch, Paris
Gilles de Chabaneix, Paris

STATE OF NEW YORK.

BY

Legislative Authority

1842

LAKE ONTARIO

LAKE ERIE

PENNSYLVANIA

SECTION FROM THE CONNECTICUT LINE TO ROXBURY IN DELAWARE CO. N.Y.

SECTION FROM JONES BEACH L.I. TO ONEONTA.

CONTENTS

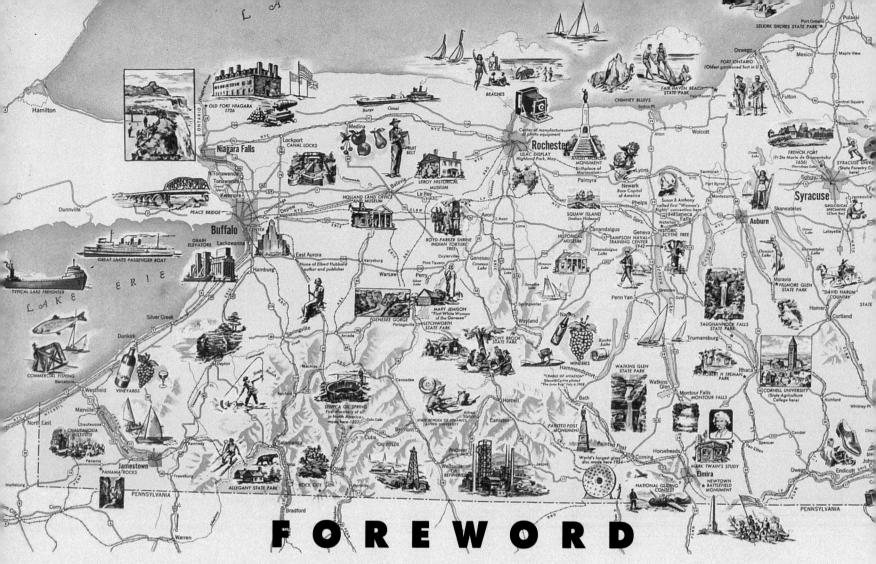

FOREWORD

by Richard F. Shepard

The phrase "New York style" conjures up, for many, visions of an overblown, concrete-cloaked life, an itchy character that thrives on impermanence. New York is not America, the national bromide has it, and I, for one, have vivid memories of being asked, in all innocence, during a western bus ride whether I lived in a "home." It may not have been much, I responded, but I certainly called it home.

Now, in the pages of *New York Style* everyone, Empire Staters and others, can witness for themselves the splendid if not unique syntheses of cultural decor that distinguish the civilization that has flourished in the Hudson Valley — from the remote fastnesses of the Adirondacks to the famed sidewalks of New York.

Can we define New York style as neatly as we can tell you what is characteristic of Provence or the American Southwest or Polynesia or other neighborhoods where societies maintained a traditional architecture and way of life to live in it? New York is a boundary state rich in "betweens." It is between New England and the Midwest, between the Old World (via the Atlantic) and the New World, between old-stock Anglo-Dutch founders and endless waves of new stock.

Small wonder that, as you travel through the lush country depicted here, you will perhaps be bemused to find that New York is a place that is always new at the same time that it is always old. New Yorkers do not behave like transients even if they are on the move; there is a compulsion among individuals to feel they are amending and not revolutionizing an environment.

You will see this in the reconstructed 200-year-old Eastfield Village, near Albany, and you will see it in the loving furnishings of a town house in Harlem's Hamilton Heights. In the Catskills is a farmhouse that has been adapted to a nonagricultural owner without sacrifice of its pristine simplicity. In New York City's East Village, a railroad flat that housed working-class immigrants in the most unadorned conditions has been transformed into a thoroughly modern habitat. Whether it is a new home aboard a refurbished old tugboat in New York harbor or a modern home in the Hamptons, there is always a nod — no, more of a deep bow — to

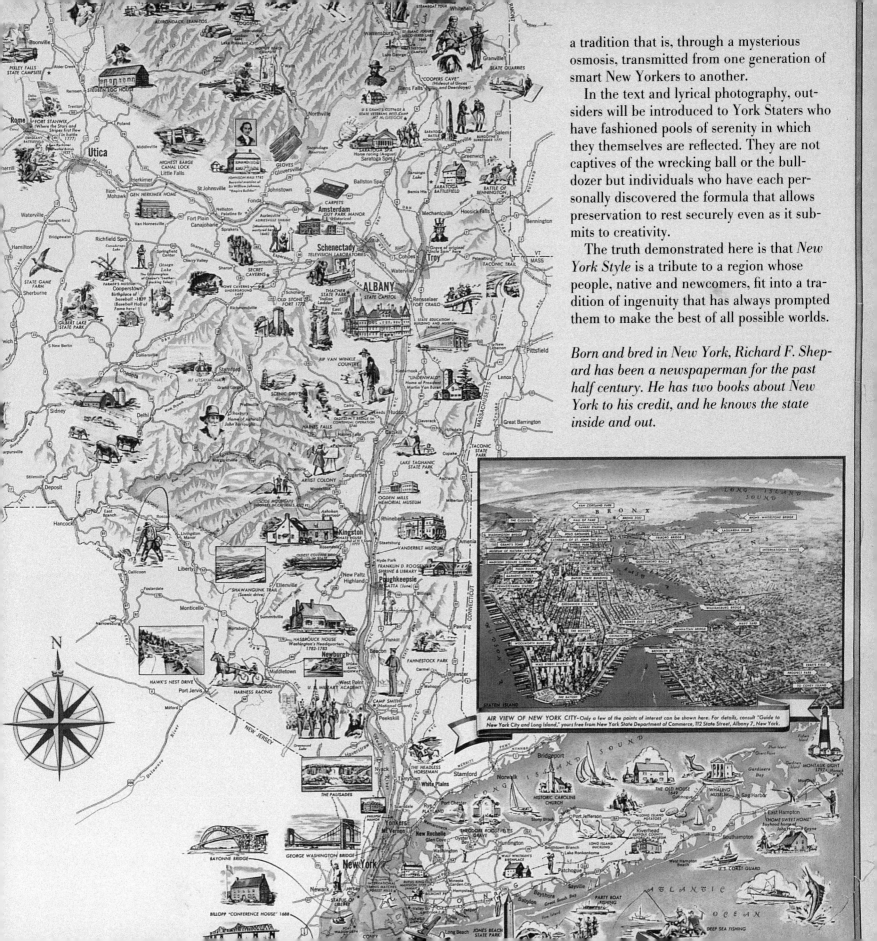

a tradition that is, through a mysterious osmosis, transmitted from one generation of smart New Yorkers to another.

In the text and lyrical photography, outsiders will be introduced to York Staters who have fashioned pools of serenity in which they themselves are reflected. They are not captives of the wrecking ball or the bulldozer but individuals who have each personally discovered the formula that allows preservation to rest securely even as it submits to creativity.

The truth demonstrated here is that *New York Style* is a tribute to a region whose people, native and newcomers, fit into a tradition of ingenuity that has always prompted them to make the best of all possible worlds.

Born and bred in New York, Richard F. Shepard has been a newspaperman for the past half century. He has two books about New York to his credit, and he knows the state inside and out.

AIR VIEW OF NEW YORK CITY—Only a few of the points of interest can be shown here. For details, consult "Guide to New York City and Long Island," yours free from New York State Department of Commerce, 112 State Street, Albany 7, New York.

INTRODUCTION

As the only New Yorker in the group who set out to put together *New York Style*, I sometimes forget that for a Londoner and two Frenchmen, coming here is visiting a foreign country.

What surprised me even more was that going beyond the island of Manhattan would prove to be for me as exciting an adventure as traveling to England, Spain, or Japan.

We began planning this book early in 1990. Exploring Brooklyn, driving to the tip of Montauk, or reaching the edge of Niagara Falls, the views of the Catskills, the majestic Hudson Valley, the rural farms, the picturesque lakes—all lay ahead.

We went north and east searching for what remained of Main Street in the small town. We drove to the Adirondacks in search of the great camps that so typified a privileged way of life at the turn of the century.

But what exactly are you looking for? This was the usual question we were asked as we started to focus on choosing the houses we wanted to include in *New York Style*.

The profusion of shelter magazines and the ever-growing number of coffee table books on decorating have weakened the image of what we considered to be the evolution not only of design styles but of the ways houses have been lived in over the years. We began our journey more than 10 years ago with a new kind of book, one in which we showed an eclectic choice of beautiful, original, and personal interiors that we felt represented the style of the times. Little by little our perception changed and we refined our choices. We were drawn to the past and its authentic places, where certain traditions remained. Progressively, we moved away from the modern design that so marked the 1980s.

In America, where people spend so much time and money on decorating—sometimes with unfelicitous results—we chose an opposite point of view. Our emotions became our antennae. We looked for houses with history, even if the owners might have moved in just a few months before. We wanted creativity, authenticity, taste, simplicity, originality, and sensitivity. We liked places where people were having fun, enjoying their homes, their gardens, their collections. And of course we insisted on style, that most elusive element.

New York Style is about New York City and New York State. We searched out the city's roots, its old neighborhoods. Upstate, we immersed ourselves in landscapes as powerful and captivating today as they were 100 years ago.

Mother Nature did not seem to be on our side. When we went to the Adirondacks to capture the landscape in its glorious fall colors, the leaves had already dropped from the trees and the first snows had dusted the birches that ringed Upper Saranac Lake.

On a July 4th outing to Montauk we met torrential rains and high winds—just what we wanted to capture the languid summery feeling of a beach cottage on the dunes!

We flew to Buffalo in early February—equipped for Antarctica, with only sleigh dogs missing to guide us on our way. We came face to face with a "heat wave"—temperatures in the 40-degree range—that was quickly dissipating one of the mildest snowfalls to hit the area in years. Icicles were dripping off rooftops and snow was melting at a fast pace as we drove through the many small towns we had hoped to photograph deep in winter.

We went to Niagara Falls as tourists. Instead of the cliché we feared, the Falls turned out to be one of the most moving spectacles of all time. We were mesmerized by its timeless appeal.

We visited dozens of houses, looking for examples to define our point of view. Sometimes, it was simply the way people created a magical decor with three times nothing, the way they reinvested themselves in the houses and rooms where they wanted to spend the rest of their lives.

We met extraordinary people who were passionate about their homes. If the houses were old, they willed them to live again. If the homes were new, they settled in with a strong sense of traditional values.

What began to emerge were places where the past blended with the present: a pristine turn-of-the-century farmhouse where vibrant paint colors harken back to the 18th century yet imbue the interior with a modern graphic feeling; a tugboat that required the patience and passion of many years of hard restoration; an authentic village where an ad hoc "mayor" has invested his whole life in making old houses, crafts, and traditions live again.

New York City proved to be an equal challenge. We were drawn not to the glass-enclosed penthouse, the soaring skyscraper, the sleek minimal loft. Instead it was the mid-19th-century brownstone, the Lower East Side tenement that intrigued us. We wanted to show the ingenuity of the unique eye, the way that people express themselves in their homes, the way they take risks to make personal style work for them.

The rustic style (which takes so many guises and has been expressed so powerfully by a handful of furniture craftsmen); the exoticism, eclecticism, and extraordinary sense of color at Olana, Frederick Edwin Church's Moorish palace on the Hudson; the taste for Victoriana or Gothic Revival objects that passionate collectors convey; and the growing need to get away to very simple places that allow us to breathe deeply . . . we felt strongly that these are some of the new directions and values that impact on the way we define style today.

Putting all these seemingly disparate places together in a book is what defines New York style at a particular point in time. In celebrating the past, as it is relived today, we were forging a modern style.

In *Here Is New York*, E. B. White writes: "It [New York] can destroy an individual, or it can fulfill him, depending a good deal on luck. No one should come to New York to live unless he is willing to be lucky."

We were.

NEW YORK ALBUM

From the monochromatic rhythm of Manhattan's water towers to the mesmerizing Niagara Falls — a sight whose timeless power takes us by surprise — New York State offers a series of memorable images: Fulton Ferry, looking charmingly out-of-place set against the dramatic panorama of city skyscrapers; tall pines silhouetted in the moonlight on Upper Saranac Lake; a crisp red airplane hangar rising from a bright green field in Watermill; the poetically blank facade of a SoHo loft building; stately Victorian houses lining a residential street in Hudson; snow dusting a dairy farm near Buffalo; and weathered wood steps leading to the beach in Bridgehampton, where open stretches of sand and sea beckon.

two
THE WAY IT WAS

Either preserved by generations of a single family, or made into a historic landmark, or willed back to life by dedicated people, many old houses have come down to us in their original states. Some are living museums and give us a glimpse of how it was, exactly — as if the original occupants had just stepped out the door. Others are more interpretative — personality-filled versions of the taste, passion, and art of living of an era that we will not see again. These are the houses that allow the past to be relived in a new way. They are our witnesses, our inspirations.

LEFT *A row of pastel-hued 19th-century brownstones parades down a tree-lined Brooklyn street.*

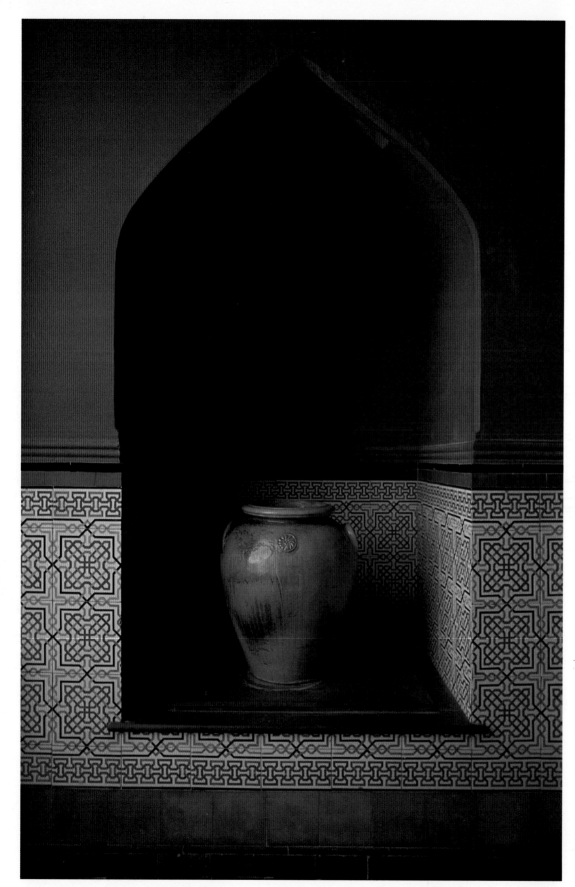

MOORISH
Fantasy on the Hudson

It took the American landscape painter Frederick Edwin Church more than twenty years to completely realize Olana, his Near Eastern castle 500 feet above the Hudson.

Church's first architect, William Morris Hunt, envisioned a French château on the dramatic site, but a trip abroad in the late 1860s left Church enthralled with Persian and Islamic architecture. In 1870 Church commissioned Calvert Vaux to interpret his ideas, which included Persian pointed arches, a polychrome facade of rubblestone quarried on the site, multicolored bricks, mosaic tiles, and roofs covered in black, green, red, and gilded slate laid in elaborate geometric patterns.

The interior is no less complex and subtle in its color harmonies than many of Church's paintings. The intense violet entrance hall opens onto the central Court Hall with its lemon-yellow walls and light blue-green ceiling. Church, inspired by ancient Middle Eastern tiles, created his own patterns on doors and archways.

Olana's exoticism is as appealing today as it was more than 100 years ago. The carefully contrived naturalistic landscape, with controlled vistas toward the extraordinary artificial lake that mirrors the shape of the river as it opens onto a lakelike expanse, was the inspiration for many of the artist's paintings. Some still hang in the intimate rooms that were lived in by Church's family until 1966, when Olana became a museum. These paintings, along with family heirlooms and mementos, combine to make Olana so full of atmosphere that it seems as if Church had just stepped out of his studio onto the porch to get a breath of fresh air.

LEFT *A blue-glazed jar stands in a niche by the front door.*

RIGHT *With its striped canvas awnings, Olana looks much the same as when it was completed in 1891.*

ABOVE *A 19th-century marble sculpture of Dorothea has been placed just inside the front door. The etched glass is original to the house.*

ABOVE RIGHT *A group of Parian statues and two marble pieces by the American artist Chauncey Bradley Ives — The Beggar Boy and Ariadne — crowd a front parlor dominated by a large Renaissance Revival cabinet. The silk damask draperies were made for the room.*

RIGHT *In the dining room, the burl walnut marble-topped sideboard holds a collection of Victorian silver and silver plate. The high-relief marble plaque of a Victorian girl dates from the latter part of the 19th century.*

SALVAGED

Buildings Near Albany

As a teenager, Don Carpentier found some old bottles but discovered he had nowhere to put them. So he made himself a small building out of pieces of salvage to house his growing collection. That was the beginning of Eastfield Village, a 16-acre compound 11 miles from Albany, where Carpentier now lives with his wife, Denise, and two children, Hannah and Jared Elias.

The original salvage building is gone, but the village now includes a 1790 residence and a 1787 workman's house, as well as a meeting house, a church, a blacksmith's shop, a tinsmith's shop, a glassworker's house, a weaver's shop, and a bevy of outhouses. It is a working laboratory of rural life as it was 200 years ago.

The authenticity extends to the furnishings — pottery, quill pens, old candlesticks. There is no electricity or indoor plumbing. In the summer students come to help restore the buildings, learn the fundamentals of different crafts, and become immersed in the past. This historic approach is Carpentier's way of understanding the present.

The imperfections of the intentionally run-down buildings, the rich textures of the walls, the well-worn objects often salvaged from other sites, and the rooms that are filled with all the activities of daily life infuse the village with a vitality that allows all who come there to experience the past firsthand and appreciate the old values made new again.

LEFT AND RIGHT *Well-worn wood, old windows, and historic houses are woven into the texture of Eastfield Village.*

ROUGHING IT

In the Adirondacks

It began more than 100 years ago when the Adirondacks became a refuge for city dwellers wanting to get away from heat and noise and pollution.

Especially in the summer months, people traveled north to sit by a lake and breathe in fresh, cool air. Most lived in modest tent sites, but the lucky few were invited to "rough it" at one of the many fashionable and luxurious millionaires' camps that were built by the most sophisticated architects of the day.

The interiors and pieces of furniture offer a tantalizing view of what it was like to summer on Raquette or Lower Saranac Lake. But more important is the interplay of furniture and nature as seen by the master craftsmen who transformed cedar and birch, or twig, root, and burl, or bark into imaginative masterpieces. This is the unique stylistic legacy of the Adirondacks.

LEFT *At dawn, against a background of mist, a duck glides across Upper Saranac Lake, one of the many extraordinary natural sites in the Adirondacks.*

TOP RIGHT AND TOP RIGHT CENTER *Birch-bark veneer and twig or log framing are among the wood techniques associated with the Adirondack style.*

ABOVE RIGHT *Cut-out red-painted shutters decorate one of the buildings at the Point, originally Camp Wonundra, home of William Avery Rockefeller on Upper Saranac Lake.*

RIGHT *Local craftsmen made the colorfully painted fretwork and trim that decorate the windows and eaves of the Russian-inspired dacha at Topridge, Marjorie Merriweather Post's camp on Upper Saint Regis Lake.*

ABOVE *Silver birch trees supplied the bark used as veneer on furniture and interior walls.*

LEFT *The dining room in the Adirondack Museum at Blue Mountain Lake has been furnished with a table and chairs that date from the first decade of the century and were crafted in Upper Saranac Lake by Ernest Stowe, a carpenter. The chairs are of yellow birch. The tabletop is inlaid with white birch bark. A late-19th-century German cooler is decorated with reindeer heads.*

BELOW LEFT *A shelf unit made by Ernest Stowe is of applied white birch bark and is trimmed with yellow birch.*

BELOW *The early-20th-century secretary came from Camp Ninomis on Upper Saranac Lake. Yellow birch has been applied to a white birch bark surface.*

ABOVE *Silver birch trees whose leaves have already fallen look etched in white against the late fall landscape.*

LEFT *The living room of Bull Cottage at the Blue Mountain Lake Museum has been furnished with an Ernest Stowe sideboard of applied white birch bark trimmed in yellow birch. The table was originally made for Sagamore Lodge at Sagamore Lake and has a top of mosaic twig crafted of striped maple, witch hazel, and birch. The base is the root of a yellow birch tree. The rocking chair has a yellow birch frame with a woven ash-splint seat and back.*

LEFT *The monumentally rugged cedar bed with an asymmetrical headboard at the Adirondack Museum was made by Joseph Bryere in Raquette Lake in 1895.*

RIGHT *A pair of snowshoes hangs under the eaves of a bedroom at the Blue Mountain Lake Museum. The Joseph Bryere dresser is a dramatic design of applied birch bark with added split-twig shadbrush. It was made in 1897 for Brightside-on-Raquette, the hotel that Bryere owned with his wife and that opened in 1891.*

LEFT *Designed by Benjamin Muncil in the 1920s, the boathouse at Topridge is a rustic masterpiece. Like many of the structures crafted from tree trunks and branches, it blends into the surrounding landscape.*

BELOW LEFT *A settee has been placed on the cedar porch of the boathouse.*

RIGHT *In the boathouse's "outdoor living room," rustic furniture is grouped around the large stone fireplace.*

ABOVE *Classic Adirondack chairs offer a tranquil spot among trees on Upper Saranac Lake.*

FAR LEFT, LEFT, AND BELOW LEFT *The various log buildings at the Point have been refurbished for use as a luxury hotel. Furnished with vintage pieces as well as newer reproductions, the rooms evoke the early times of the Adirondack camps.*

RIGHT *Rustic chairs — of birch and cedar, hickory and willow, twig and log — in a variety of techniques hint at the range of virtuosity of the Adirondack craftsmen. When made of slats, the chair has now come to be known as the classic Adirondack, although it has not been proven to be indigenous to the area. Originally made to be used out of doors, the chairs were moved indoors to heighten the rustic feeling of the lodges.*

three
THE CITY SCENE

There are some people for whom living in the city involves making a commitment to its past. These are not Manhattanites who choose the view from the 40th floor. Rather, these are people who prefer to be by places that signified home for generations past. It may not be easy. Some of the most architecturally significant houses require a serious, ongoing commitment to make them livable again. But all over New York are places where high ceilings, remnants of plaster moldings and carved fireplaces, the possibility of having even part of what was once a whole house for one's own presents just the right challenge.

LEFT *A former department store, this cast-iron building in Manhattan's Chelsea area dates from the 1870s.*

FRENCH STYLE,
American Apartment

One would be more likely to come across the rare Louis XV carved and painted beechwood chair, with its original paint and its high hinged back — a *fauteuil à razer*, or shaving chair — in a museum setting than in the guest bedroom of a family apartment. But Susan and Anthony Victoria's apartment in New York's Dakota Apartments — designed by Henry J. Hardenbergh in 1884 — is an exception. Since 1981 — when the couple moved into the high-ceilinged rooms with their two young children, Asheley and Freddy — they have created an environment where great antiques can exist in an atmosphere of informality.

Frederick Victoria — Anthony's father, and like him an antiques dealer — lived in half the rooms since the 1960s. When the couple acquired the adjoining space 10 years ago, father and son restored the apartment back to its original grandeur.

Many elements — including the extraordinary carved wood draperies crafted by a German carver, the French marble mantelpieces, and the tall French antique cabinets for which the apartment was chosen in the first place — were retained.

84

The generously proportioned rooms provided the perfect setting for two generations of collecting. The present arrangement, with its uncluttered groupings of precious objects, gives the space a playful look. Rather than intimidating, the fine antiques become approachable, and, as they were centuries ago, part of a family's everyday, albeit very stylish, lifestyle.

ABOVE LEFT *The 100-year-old Dakota Apartment Building is a Manhattan landmark.*

FAR LEFT *In the foyer, a miniature Règence bergère stands on an 18th-century faux marbre chest. Mufflers and gloves are kept in the drawers so they can be picked up easily on the way out the front door. The mirror is a late-18th-century Sicilian overdoor panel. The floor is parquet de Versailles inlaid with marble.*

ABOVE AND RIGHT *The five-legged Louis XV shaving chair — with its hinged back that drops down so wigs could be powdered — dates from about 1775 and sits in a corner of the guest room. The walls are upholstered in gray flannel and the bed is of steel and bronze. The chinoiserie painting dates from the 18th century. The green-stained ivory clock is a 19th-century version of an 18th-century clock by Martin Carlin.*

ABOVE *A piece of antique textile and a late-18th-century trompe l'oeil painting of an engraving with broken glass and a fly sit in the living room on a Louis XV chaise d'amour.*

LEFT *A comfortable sofa and piles of books add an air of informality to the large living room. The Venetian-style mirror over the French Louis XV marble antique mantelpiece was added to emphasize the European feeling of the room. The rock crystal lamps are adaptations of one Frederick Victoria bought in the 1950s.*

ABOVE *In the living room, a polychromed terra-cotta stove that dates from about 1780 stands between the windows. The overscale French mid-18th-century oak cabinet came from the collection of Baron Cassel.*

ABOVE *A photograph of Asheley Victoria is propped up on the 18th-century inlaid marble mantelpiece in the small sitting room.*

ABOVE *A Venetian chinoiserie figure representing Autumn is in front of the window of the small sitting room. The clock is from the Louis XVI period.*

ABOVE *A mercury glass ball is the centerpiece on the marble-topped table in the small sitting room. The draperies are of carved and painted wood.*

LEFT *In the dining room, a set of 19th-century Italian garden chairs that once belonged to Condé Nast surrounds the table. The trompe l'oeil wainscoting resembles a series of exotic marbles. The 18th-century Louis XVI door came from a boiserie the Victorias once owned. The Venetian chinoiserie figure representing Spring serenely stands by.*

ABOVE *The original sliding oak pocket doors date from the late 19th century, when the Dakota was built. They have been stripped and opened to reveal an early Venetian carved wood bench in the hall.*

TRIBECA

Loft Conversion

The 7,000-square-foot space in the TriBeCa section of New York City was once the corporate headquarters of the American Thread Company, whose 1896 building was designed by architect William B. Tubby as the American Wool Exchange.

Converted into apartments in the mid-eighties, the loft building offered Etro, an Italian textile company, just what it was looking for in New York: a large, dramatic, top-floor space for a showroom and a private residence that still retained many architectural details from its past. In spite of mosaic floors and baronial fireplaces and a round paneled boardroom topped with a stained-glass cupola, the most luxurious aspect was the expanse of the space itself.

Instead of cluttering it, the owners imaginatively furnished the space with overscaled European antiques, mostly from the Art

Deco period, and huge Italian paintings, creating a counterpoint to the turn-of-the-century American Victorian rooms.

Most striking is the rotunda, where a massive table stands alone, a symbol of the powerful pull of grand space in the urban landscape.

ABOVE AND RIGHT *The majestic rotunda still retains its 100-year-old mosaic floor, curved pocket doors, and wood paneling. The hardware that supported gas lamps is still there. A mid-19th-century English walnut table is nine feet in diameter, yet is dwarfed by the room.*

ABOVE LEFT *The American Thread Building has a distinctive curved facade.*

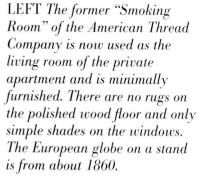

LEFT *The former "Smoking Room" of the American Thread Company is now used as the living room of the private apartment and is minimally furnished. There are no rugs on the polished wood floor and only simple shades on the windows. The European globe on a stand is from about 1860.*

LEFT *The English Victorian chairs have been reupholstered with a woven wool-and-cotton fabric manufactured by Etro. The molding on the ceiling is original, as is all the oak paneling.*

RIGHT *The bed and wall cabinet in the guest room are from the 1930s. The bed of parchment was made by Piacentini.*

RIGHT *On the stand is a 1920s painting by Alfred Egerton Cooper,* Woman in White Silk.

LEFT *In the guest bedroom a small marquetry table that came from a church stands between two pencil drawings — studies for lacquered screens by Jean Dunand.*

BELOW FAR LEFT *The 1940s Italian ceramic sculpture of a skyscraper is silhouetted against Manhattan commercial buildings.*

BELOW LEFT *A set of oak-and-steel furniture made in Austria in the 1920s is in the kitchen. The painting was bought on a street in New York City.*

RIGHT *The huge half-moon-shaped painting in the showroom is a 1926 work by Traverso Mattia titled* The Triumph of the Sea. *It was bought especially for the space. The parchment, bronze, and yellow marble table is by Busini Vici, an Italian architect who worked in Rome in the 1930s.*

HISTORIC
House in Hamilton Heights

It was about seven years ago that interior designers Timothy Van Dam and Ronald Wagner bought an 1896 townhouse in Hamilton Heights, one of Harlem's most historic neighborhoods.

Over the years, the five-story François I–style residence, designed by Clarence True, had been turned into a rooming house for a dozen or so tenants—quite a change from its beginnings as home to Dr. Ernest J. Lederle, a New York City health commissioner and founder of a large pharmaceutical company.

Like many of the area's most recent residents, Van Dam and Wagner found that in Harlem they could afford to buy a house with gracious proportions and elegant details and have money left over for the necessary restoration. The electrical and plumbing work took up most of their initial budget, leaving them time to decide how to reinstate some of the house's original grandeur.

Even though both owners are avid collectors of antiques, they have infused many of the classically ornamented rooms with an air of informality and a sense of levity.

LEFT *The staircase rises from the ground floor to an arcaded hall with a marble floor. The oculus has been painted in a trompe l'oeil cloud design. A porcelain bird cage with stuffed crows stands on the grand piano.*

BELOW *Painted a serene sage green and accented with a gilded molding, the living room contains many unusual furnishings— most found in antiques shops and thrift stores in Harlem. The Neoclassical fireplace with its onyx surround is original to the house. Simple muslin draperies cover the windows.*

TOP LEFT *A small seat has been built into the staircase on the parlor floor.*

TOP RIGHT *A 19th-century painting of an exotic Near Eastern dancer is on the bedroom-floor landing.*

ABOVE AND RIGHT *An assortment of Neoclassical elements, including columns, obelisks, and statuary, are juxtaposed with industrial metal shelving in the second-floor library. The pair of leather-and-mahogany armchairs was designed by architect Joseph H. Frank Freedlander in 1909. The red damask draperies came from a church thrift shop on Park Avenue South. Van Dam made the model of New York City's Beaux Arts police building as a student project.*

LEFT AND BELOW FAR LEFT
The walls in the master bedroom retain the distressed blue-and-white treatment found throughout the house in its days as a rooming house. John Kelley painted the portraits of the two owners. An Oriental carpet and a chinchilla throw drape a 19th-century chaise longue lighted by a 1920s iron floor lamp with a parchment shade.

BELOW LEFT *The marble washbasin, claw-footed bathtub, and tiles with a sea-horse-and-shell motif are vintage elements in the master bathroom. A Gothic Revival hall chair and Victorian lantern add to the authentic period look.*

RIGHT *A 1909 life drawing of a male figure from the Pennsylvania Academy of Fine Art is set on the fireplace andirons in the master bedroom. A pair of tole chestnut roasters, family photographs, and an ostrich egg decorate the mantel.*

f o u r
THE COUNTRY LIFE

Living in the country — if only for the weekend — supposes a return to simple values, to natural materials, to the idea of the hand-made. The country is a place where the garden, the house, the furnishings all take time to come into their own. For some, the country is a return to very rustic houses; for others, more contemporary luxuries are deemed necessary. The old-time big kitchen filled with all the old-time things — McCoy bowls, rows of canned tomatoes, spatterware, wooden spoons — is where friends and family gather. But the New York country style supposes a certain level of sophistication with the inclusion of unusual folk art, Early American antiques, even contemporary paintings.

LEFT *An old barn near Westfield is painted a classic dark red.*

FEDERAL
Family Home

Built in 1815, the Federal house with its three barns had barely been touched until Jason McCoy and Diana Burroughs, New York art dealers, decided to make the Cooperstown house a weekend and summer retreat for themselves and their three young children, Sanford, Jackson, and Samantha Clare.

The couple fell for the house because of its run-down but essentially pristine condition. Nevertheless, they took about a year and a half to renovate the property.

Keeping the original doors and windows intact, as well as the random wide-plank floors, they added four fireplaces — as well as a second floor to the ell, some bathrooms, a kitchen, three children's bedrooms, a playroom, and a deck modeled after that at Jefferson's house in Monticello.

While designers Christopher Smallwood and Alain Mertens worked on the exterior, Jacques Dehornois helped with the interior — where the walls and trim were painted in authentic Colonial colors and where the unusual furnishings, mostly antiques, are placed sparingly and dramatically in the spacious rooms.

LEFT *A tall maple, one of many on the property, shades the 1815 house.*

ABOVE RIGHT AND CENTER RIGHT *The renovation included adding a deck inspired by Jefferson's Monticello and relocating the front door to its original position.*

RIGHT *Plans for the future include restoring the old barns to their original condition and raising animals.*